Business Beyond
Base Camp

Business Beyond Base Camp

A Tale for Business Leaders

Bernard Johann Putz, Ph.D.

iUniverse, Inc.
New York Lincoln Shanghai

Business Beyond Base Camp
A Tale for Business Leaders

iUniverse books may be ordered through booksellers or by contacting:

iUniverse
2021 Pine Lake Road, Suite 100
Lincoln, NE 68512
www.iuniverse.com
1-800-Authors (1-800-288-4677)

This is a work of fiction. Names, characters, places, and incidents
either are the product of the author's imagination or are used
fictitiously. Any resemblance to actual persons, living or dead, business
establishments, events, or locales, is entirely coincidental.

ISBN: 0-595-32294-8 (Pbk)
ISBN: 0-595-66512-8 (Cloth)

Printed in the United States of America

To my wife, Dagmar, whose vision for me often surpasses my own and whose constant support made this novel possible. And to my young son, Adrian, who teaches me to look at my own leadership behavior every day.

Contents

Introduction

Business Beyond Base Camp is a novel with an important message about leading an organization to the next level. "Dirk," a fictional CEO, is frustrated by the growing pains of his business. To get his mind off work, he joins a twenty-five day trek through the rugged mountains of Nepal. The group's guide is Roger, a former CEO, who successfully led two companies through several difficult transitions. During the trek, Dirk finds time to reflect and realizes that the nature of his business, as well as the people who run it, including himself, must change.

Although a fictional story, this book is based on close to twenty years of observing and advising executives who have managed similar transitions. It is written as a novel to help executives obtain practical insights that they can implement Monday morning. Even more importantly, it is written to help them understand the personal and behavioral changes necessary in leading such a change. Since a transition of this nature is invariably strategic, operational, and cultural, executives need to change their leadership practices to ensure that improvement efforts take root in day-to-day operations.

Business Beyond Base Camp was written primarily for CEOs and senior management of growing companies. However, general managers and executives of larger corporations have also found these principles helpful in improving the performance of their business units or divisions. What leaders do, or do not do, is pivotal in successfully taking a business to the next stage of growth. Too often, changes in work processes, strategic direction, or operations fail because executives do not change how they lead; or they do not change the organizational systems to reinforce the "new way of doing things." This book attempts to provide a deeper, more intuitive understanding of the personal, operational, and organizational challenges of business growth.

Those who wish to read from cover to cover can do so in a matter of hours. Those who want "just the facts" can jump to the end of each chapter where Dirk captures his insights in a personal journal. Although they are not presented in any particular sequence, all the insights are important to help a business move forward. As you read, I encourage you to reflect on your own business experience and to write the implications in the available space.

So, enjoy the story as you learn more about how to take your business to the next level of success in *Business Beyond Base Camp*!

Author

Dr. Bernard J. Putz has worked with executives of Fortune 500 companies, as well as with executives of multi-million dollar businesses to address their most significant growing pains. He helps senior executives take an integrated perspective, advising them on the specific leadership practices critical for operational excellence and making good, fast, strategic decisions.

Dr. Putz is the founder of Next Level Leadership, a consulting, coaching, and education firm that helps executives take their business to the next level of growth. He is also a co-founder of Peritus Precision Translations, Inc., an agency that offers high quality translation services and global brand name analyses for over seventy languages. He has an MA and Ph.D. in Organizational Psychology from the California School of Organization Studies at Alliant International University and an MBA from Notre Dame de Namur University. He began his career working with Silicon Valley companies, implementing the management practices necessary to decrease time-to-market. He then moved to Motorola to help integrate Six Sigma Quality and 10X Reduction in Cycle Time Initiatives into the day-to-day operating practices of various business units. Later he spent several years at both Cap Gemini/Ernst & Young and Deloitte Consulting, helping clients address the leadership practices necessary to improve implementation, execution, and cross-functional integration. He has written several articles as well as another book, *Designing Cross Functional Business Processes*. Bernard can be reached at bernard@nl-leadership.com or on his website at www.nl-leadership.com.

Main Characters

Dirk is the CEO who is struggling with his business's growing pains and who would like to take his company to the next level.

Roger is the mountain guide and leader of the Nepal Trek. He is the former CEO of two successful companies that he had led through similar transitions, turning them into multi-billion dollar corporations.

Bikram is the Sridar, the Sherpa mountain guide, who manages the other Sherpas, porters, and kitchen assistants.

Marianne, Beth, Marshall, Larry, Sam, Lisa, Karl, and Carlos join Dirk as members of Roger's trekking party.

Ralph, Phil, George, and Monica are a second trekking party.

Chapter 1

Before the Departure

Silicon Valley, California

Dirk gets home late, as usual, finishing a voicemail as he pulls into the driveway. He wanders into the house pre-occupied with the last minute changes in the quarterly numbers and with an irate customer call.

His wife Mary is still up reading. After a quick hello, he settles onto the couch with a sigh of relief. In the middle of his usual recital of the day's events, he abruptly changes topics. "I don't know if I should take this trip. Twenty-five days away from the office is a lot."

Mary sighs and looks into his eyes, "You can't change plans now. You've wanted this for a long time."

"I know. There's just so much happening. We're constantly fighting fires and things are falling through the cracks. I feel as if I'm missing something."

"Not thinking about work for a while will give you a new perspective."

"I am looking forward to the trek with Roger. He's leading the group. You remember Roger?"

Mary, tilting her head, "Wasn't he the former CEO we met at that industry party a couple of years ago?"

"Yes. He got tired of the corporate jungle and now leads treks throughout the world."

The next day Roger calls. The trip is still several weeks away, but he would like to get together with Dirk and Mary to discuss the details. He wants to get to know them better and to understand what Dirk hopes to achieve with this trip. He is talking with each of the trekkers ahead of time.

Roger suggests that since this is Dirk's first trip, he may want to call others who have traveled with him before. A few days later, Dirk finds time to call three people.

Later in the evening, Dirk describes the conversations to Mary. "Each person I talked to was uncommonly enthusiastic. I asked all of them if they had been on other treks. They said they had. But since going with Roger, they won't use anyone else, even though others cost less. Some have traveled with him all around the world."

"Isn't that a bit dangerous? Is he familiar with the terrain in all those areas?"

"They said he surrounds himself with experts whenever he can."

Mary is visibly relieved that her husband seems to be in good hands.

"Sam, the guy I talked to on the phone, said that Roger goes out of his way to ensure the entire experience is spectacular. He can anticipate people's needs and is prepared for the unexpected. By the way, did I tell you he's coming over Friday?"

"Yes, you did mention it."

A few days later, Friday evening, Roger is on time.

Mary opens the door with a cheery "Hi. You must be Roger?" She now recognizes the 6'3", tanned, former CEO, whose looks give no indication of his 65 years.

"Yes, I must," he says, with a pleasant smile as he hands her a bottle from his private vineyard.

"C'mon in," she says. "Dirk's still at the office wrapping up last minute details. He should be here any minute."

"I remember those days."

Just as the door closes, Dirk screeches into the driveway, barking orders into his cell phone.

"...And make sure that manufacturing line gets up and running by next week. If he can't do it, get him help. Heads are going to roll if I hear any more bad news."

He slams the phone shut and walks through the door.

"Hi Roger, how are you?"

"Good, but more importantly, how are you?"

"I'm fine, except for constantly putting out fires."

"Fires?"

"In the last hour, I learned we launched a new product with half the support material not ready. Now we're scrambling to prepare our biggest distributors, after the fact. We still haven't finished the manufacturing process for the new line. It was supposed to be complete already. Our biggest European customer wants samples by the end of the week."

"Oh, I can just imagine. I know there's a lot on your mind about the business. But tonight, I'd like to talk to you and Mary about Nepal and our upcoming trek."

Throughout the evening, Roger carefully observes the interaction between Dirk and Mary. He also becomes aware of their habits and interests. After some small talk, they sit down to a wonderful meal of swordfish, broccoli, wild rice, and a fine bottle of Chardonnay. During dinner, Roger asks Dirk why he chose this trip to Nepal, and why now? Roger's questions are probing— everything from what led Dirk to make this decision to how Mary feels about the trip.

After finishing the last morsel of fish, they continue the conversation in the living room. Roger explains that his goal is to ensure that each trekker has the ultimate trekking experience. For some this is a once in a lifetime event; for others it is one of many. No surprise to Mary, the conversation soon shifts back to work. Dirk continues to vent about his concerns and problems. It is clear that he is not fully focused on the trip. Mary is all too familiar with her husband's inability to turn off the office.

Roger listens intently, throwing in the occasional question. Sensing Dirk's preoccupation with work and recognizing that this will not change during a twenty-five day trip, Roger makes a suggestion. "It's going to be tough for you to get your mind off work.

I realize a vacation now can be distracting and even difficult emotionally. Especially, given the current situation. What has worked with others is to have time to bounce around ideas. I'd be happy to be your sounding board."

Dirk appreciates Roger's gesture and soon the evening ends. Roger says his goodbyes and heads off.

Dirk and Mary get ready for bed. Dirk with a mouthful of toothpaste says, "What an interesting evening. Roger asked so many questions."

"He did. I liked that," Mary says.

"Why do you say that?"

"I'd say he spent ninety percent of the time listening. He really got to know us—your goals for the trek, our interests, and my expectations."

Dirk stares at a point in the mirror. "It seems like he was trying to look at everything from our perspective. I was surprised how comfortable I felt telling him things."

"Me, too." In a thoughtful tone Mary continues, "I think it's his sense of humility. He didn't try to sell us on his treks. He wanted to know about you. He really cares about his customers—and he seems so approachable."

As they both sit on the edge of the bed, Mary teases Dirk on how he can learn something from Roger. Dirk, always struggling to get his mind off the day-to-day pressures, naturally begins to think about how Mary's comments could affect the business. He takes out his journal, the one that has been buried in his nightstand for months, leans back, and scribbles a few notes.

First Insight

Empathy is at the heart of customer loyalty.

- ➤ Force yourself to "walk in your customer's shoes."
  - Appreciate the entire customer experience.
- ➤ Instill a customer-centric mindset.
  - Ensure unfiltered, on-going, customer feedback.
  - Understand why customers will or won't tell you their biggest concerns.
- ➤ Understand why customers are loyal.
  - Measure more than satisfaction.
  - Determine why or why not customers will do business with you even in the face of attractive alternatives.
  - Understand why or why not customers will enthusiastically recommend your business to their colleagues and friends.
  - Track progress on actions that improve customer loyalty.

Notes

....

....

....

....

....

....

....

....

....

....

....

....

....

....

Chapter 2

The Hotel in Kathmandu

A couple of weeks after Roger's dinner with Dirk and Mary, the trekkers all meet at the Hyatt in Kathmandu, the hub of Nepal's economy and the gateway to backcountry trekking adventures. The city is filled with bicycles, noisy mopeds, and cars reeking of diesel fumes. It's such a clash between old and new. Unmarked streets, decrepit buildings, interspersed with rose-brick temples, and new construction makes getting around this city a challenge.

Different from most treks, which tend to assemble and then head straight into the countryside, Roger's group spends the first day in Kathmandu. Individuals have the morning free to explore the city. The afternoon and evening will be spent getting to know one another, talking about what it means to be a team, and reviewing the itinerary. While individuals tour the city, Roger takes care of visa procedures and border formalities. He also arranges for a liaison officer to accompany the group in restricted areas.

Right after lunch the group meets in one of the hotel meeting rooms. Roger asks the Sirdar, Bikram, the leader of the Sherpas, to join them as well. Roger turns to the group. "Why don't we start with introductions? Take ten minutes to tell us about yourself, your background, interests, and your definition of a successful trek."

Marianne, Beth, Marshall, and Larry have trekked on shorter and easier tours in the Himalayas before. Sam and Lisa have never been to the Himalayas but are experienced mountaineers. They have climbed several North American and European peaks. Carlos has hiked in the Sierras and knows his way around the backcountry.

Least experienced are Karl and Dirk, who have kept in shape, with trips to the gym and shorter hikes.

As the introductions finish, Marshall asks, "Roger. In the introductory package you sent, there were two additional people. They aren't here today."

Dirk has noticed the same thing, but does not think much of it. He figures that people have just cancelled. Little does he know that Roger has rarely had a cancellation.

"Good question, Marshall. I spent time with each of you individually. After those conversations, I looked at the entire team and decided if all the people were appropriate, given our trip. Two people didn't fit."

Marshall presses, "Why?"

"I don't want to go into it in great detail, but we're going to be at high altitudes and exerting ourselves with difficult climbs. They weren't ready. Turns out one had a heart condition, and the other had never been hiking. I suggested they take a simpler seven-day trek in one of the lower valleys around Kathmandu."

Everyone understands Roger's rationale. Dirk, a bit surprised how carefully Roger has screened the participants, thinks that people have just signed up, gotten a guide, and off they went. Not the case with Roger.

Roger pulls the group back on track by focusing on the next agenda item. "Let's move on. I want to cover how we need to work together. This is critical to a successful trek."

Beth, having traveled on less adventurous treks, is skeptical. "Is this really necessary? No group I've been with has ever done this before."

Interrupting Roger, Marshall replies, "Given our itinerary, we need to be clear about how we work as a team. On another trek that was less strenuous, with a lot less risk, people just couldn't pull together. We had to leave out a lot of interesting activities because people couldn't rely on each other to come through. The mood was terrible. It was a long fourteen days."

Those who have a comparison with other treks are all ready to chime in and help explain the importance of this prep work. Roger, sensing that this could be a long diversion, focuses the group back on team ground rules. "We need to agree to some basic rules for how we intend to work together. Once we agree, I expect all of us to hold each other accountable to these rules—starting today."

Dirk whispers to Marshall, "So, what's he going to do if somebody doesn't?"

"He'll ask you to leave."

"What? You've got to be kidding."

Marshall tells the story of another trek during which someone would not follow the agreed upon rules. She would agree to decisions, and then do her own thing, looking out only for herself. She didn't want to work as a team and did not communicate openly. On several climbs, people's lives depended on one another. Trust levels were going down. Roger confronted the woman several times, but nothing changed. So, on the fifth day, he asked her to leave and join a group that was returning to Kathmandu. The group was thankful that Roger dealt with the situation. Had he not, it would have cast doubt on his leadership ability. That day he sent a strong message about what he is willing to accept and not accept.

Dirk and Marshall return their attention to the group just as Roger says, "The first rule is that we consider the safety of ourselves and of the group in everything we do. The second is that we have open and honest discussions as a group. We put issues on the table and talk about 'undisscussables,' the issues that everyone knows are there but that no one wants to mention. We don't have the time or luxury not to be candid."

The group continues to talk about how they will work together, and they agree to seven basic ground rules. They review the specifics of the itinerary and go over supplies. Bikram then outlines his role and that of the Sherpas. As the afternoon ends, Roger

describes how even though individuals have their own responsibilities and goals, success is measured by how well the entire group
does, not just one individual. He expects them to help one another. They are all affected by one another's decisions, so they need to
keep the entire team in mind, including the Sherpas.

Roger concludes, "Enough of the itinerary and 'how we work."
Dinner is at six, so feel free to do whatever you like for the rest of
the day."

Several team members take the opportunity to explore
Kathmandu's alley markets, narrow streets, and temples. Dirk and
Sam visit Durbar Square, which holds the palaces of the Malla and
Shah Kings. As they pass several temples, they keep an eye out for
the aggressive monkeys. Sam asks, "So what do you think so far?"

"Interesting. There's a lot of emphasis on the itinerary and how
Roger expects us to work together."

"The first time I was skeptical, too. Now, knowing what I do
about Roger's treks, I'm thankful."

"Why do you say thankful?" asks Dirk.

"Roger's treks are legendary. We do amazing things on these
trips and often with less experienced people. Cross ice fields with
deep crevasses. Walk on knife-edge ridges. Climb to spectacular
lookout points. This can be done because people trust each other,
communicate openly and honestly, and pull together. He can take
these risks because he builds a strong team. Everyone looks out for
one another."

"That's probably why his treks surpass the competition."

"Yeah and there's a paradox. You'd think focusing on the team
excludes the individual; but in reality if the team succeeds, so does
the individual. As a photographer I've received a lot of recognition
for my pictures, but I couldn't have gotten the shots without the
help of others."

Sam and Dirk explore the palaces and temples and then head
back to the hotel. Dirk excuses himself and heads up to his room.
His mind is filled with Sam's comments and the implication for

his business. He reclines on the bed, pulls out his journal, and writes down a few thoughts.

Second Insight

The team at the top must lead as one based on a clear itinerary.

➢ Make sure you have the right players on the team.

- Confront specific behaviors directly.

- Act decisively and quickly.

- Ensure that individuals are in the right job.

➢ Ensure a clear direction.

- Ensure everyone is clear about the vision, mission, and how to get there (strategies).

➢ Clearly communicate your expectations of how the executive team will work together.

- Create an environment of trust, open and honest communication.

- Discuss business-wide or cross-functional issues as an executive team, not in a series of one-on-one conversations.

- Build a team day-in/day-out. It's how you operate together, when you get together.

➢ Ensure that individuals look beyond their own goals and boundaries.

- Expect individuals to look at what they do and how it affects the entire team. Realize that collaboration often needs to be mandated.

- Understand what reinforces integration across boundaries and what undermines it (e.g., goals, rewards).

- Create shared goals/metrics to reinforce collaboration.

Notes

....

....

....

....

....

....

....

....

....

....

....

....

....

....

Chapter 3

Reflections from the Rooftop

Dinner is a wonderful introduction to Nepali cuisine. It consists of Bhenta Tareko, a grilled eggplant marinated with fresh Nepali herbs; Pharsi-ko Rash, a pumpkin soup with coriander; and Luiche Rana Pariwar, chicken breast marinated in light Nepali spices with cashew paste and saffron. Roger facilitates a few fun activities to help people get to know one another better. After dessert, consisting of Dudha-ko Parikar, a thick milk-roll soaked in sugar with pistachios and saffron, the group breaks up. Tomorrow is a six am start.

Dirk stows a few items in his hotel room. He's still unable to sleep and decides to head to the rooftop lounge. There, sitting in an oversized chair, is Roger staring out into the night sky. His reflection bounces off the six-foot high windows. He's talking with Bikram, the Sridar.

Pulling up another chair, Dirk says, "Hi. Mind if I join you?"

"No, not at all. We're just talking about our itinerary and the various side trips."

Dirk continues, "I'm looking forward to getting out into the backcountry. I've read the itinerary several times, but it didn't come alive until this afternoon."

"Bikram and I were just discussing our final climb to the summit. At more than six thousand meters, over 21,000 feet, it's one of the highest trekking peaks in Nepal. I've been there only once. Luckily, we have Bikram. He's been to the summit several times."

Roger and Bikram spend a few more minutes discussing last minute details. Then Bikram heads off to make sure that the jeeps will be ready first thing tomorrow morning.

Dirk notices that Roger has returned to gazing out the window. "Roger, you seem a bit distracted."

"Not really. Just reflecting."

"May I ask about what?"

"Thinking about what I have to do to make this trip successful."

"What makes you say that?"

"I was thinking about a trip years ago. I led a group high into the Andes. We were hiking up to Machu Picchu. It's a steep hike with a few treacherous sections of the trail. I had led a few treks by then and felt confident I knew everything I needed to know. There were a few issues with the group. They didn't quite gel. But it wasn't anything I couldn't handle."

"I get a sense of where this is going," Dirk chimes in.

"I didn't know it at the time, but I didn't deal with a few issues when I should have. One day, I thought we could easily cover the distance in about six hours; but in reality, it took us almost ten. Night had fallen and we were still on the trail with no place to make camp. All of a sudden, I hear the crunch of rocks giving way and a scream behind me. One of the guys had stepped on a lose rock in the dark and twisted his ankle pretty badly. He couldn't walk very well, and we were still on the trail. Luckily, there was a clear night sky. But, the whole group was at risk."

Dirk listens intently, "I assume you made it to camp safely."

"We did. The mood of the team was a mixture of gratitude for having made it and frustration with how we were operating. You could have cut the tension with a knife. And a lot was directed at me, as their guide."

"But it wasn't just you. It seems like individuals had a lot of issues with each other."

"They did. And their inability to work together frustrated me. There was another group camping on the same plateau led by a seasoned guide, whom I had met several times before. So I took him aside and explained my anger and frustration."

"Good that you had someone to vent to."

"And vent I did. He listened patiently and then very philosophically said, 'Carl Jung, the psychologist once said, 'Everything that irritates us of others can lead us to an understanding of ourselves.'"

Dirk murmurs out loud, "That's an interesting quote?"

Roger continues, "The other guide said, 'As I listen to you that quote came to mind. For ten minutes, you have talked about how individuals are not doing this or that, and how you wish they would just step up. What do you see as your role in this?'

I was a bit defensive and said, 'I'm trying to ensure they perform, make sure we have a safe trek.'"

"The guide continued, 'That may be true, but you are part of that team and your actions, more than anything else, influence their behavior.'"

"So I asked the guide, 'Are you telling me I'm the problem?' He was very blunt and to the point. 'Not exclusively, but you're part of it.'"

"That night in the Andes, I realized something. The reason the group acted the way it did was because of what I did, or in this case, didn't do."

"But you couldn't have known this was going to happen."

"Probably not. But I never clarified my expectations of how I wanted them to work together. No clear ground rules. I didn't role model the behavior I wanted. I dealt with them one-on-one and not as a team. To some extent, I abdicated, letting the group manage itself. But that wasn't realistic. They could give input, but they needed someone to set the boundaries. We needed to get better at making decisions as a group. They were all peers. Individuals couldn't make decisions for the whole group. I was the one with the authority."

Dirk in a supportive tone added, "You may be a bit hard on yourself. But I can understand there is a fine line between micromanaging a group on one hand, and abdicating on the other. I see it, too. I often see managers say I'm empowering my team; but they don't really give them the authority, so it's seen less as empowerment and more that the leader does not want to make a decision."

"Yeah, but it was also something else the other guide mentioned. He said, 'Roger. You are the director of a play. You have to honestly assess the strengths and weaknesses of the people on your trek, and most importantly the strengths and weaknesses of yourself. In the best plays, performers and directors know their limits and take it right up to the edge. Learning how to push it a little and get better every time. That can't happen if you're not aware of yourself. From that point on, I realized I have to look in the mirror every time I aspire to lead a group to a higher plateau or to a new mountain. If I want to lead the group, and not hand the role of guide to someone else, I have to ask myself what I have to do differently. What are my assumptions? What are my limitations?"

Dirk slowly nods, "What do you mean by assumptions."

"Let me tell you the story of another trek." Roger describes how he led a small group up Mount Kilimanjaro to the Shire Plateau. They had to cross a steep ridge before turning west into the river gorge. The two local guides had said that a recent mudslide had made the trail up to the ridge inaccessible. In the past, one of Roger's assumptions was that you never question the advice of a local guide. His assumption was that guides always know best and challenging them would be of little value. So they took another route, which took an additional two days, only to find out later that the pass was open. The guides had not been through that particular pass in months.

His assumption of never challenging local guides, because they were the experts, or because it might create conflict within the team, had a negative impact on the performance of the entire Kilimanjaro trek. Roger explained that by revisiting his assumptions he then realized he had to interject more inquiry into the discussions, even if this meant an increase in tension and conflict. He had to test others' assertions, in a way, help them expose their own assumptions. In other words, instead of treating interpretations as facts, help others look at interpretations as hypotheses that may need further testing. Had he done that, he would have learned that the guides had not been through that pass for months.

Dirk nods as he listens to Roger and thinks of similar situations in his own life.

It's now late in the evening, and they have an early start the next morning. Roger and Dirk finish their sweet milk tea, which will surely put them to sleep, and head down to their rooms. As Dirk settles into bed, he takes out his journal. He finds himself eager to jot down his thoughts. Even one day away from the daily grind, his thinking is getting clearer, and he is finding time to contemplate the events of the day and to realize how they connect to his life back home and to the business.

Third Insight

Leaders need to take an honest look in the mirror.

➤ Reflect on how your behaviors affect your management team and the organization.

- Accept and address your strengths and weaknesses.

- Question your assumptions and how they affect your behaviors.

- Address the three to four behaviors that may need to change to reach the next level.

- Strike a balance between micromanagement and abdication.

➤ Recognize the importance of honesty and frankness.

- Honesty won't occur without trust.

- Understand it is not about popularity.

- Pretend candor keeps people from learning.

- Interject more inquiry into discussions.

- Create a culture where interpretations are seen as hypotheses that need to be tested, not facts.

➤ Make sure you are passionate about wanting to address both the behavioral and operational issues.

- Realize this is hard work and often outside an executive's comfort zone.

- Recognize it will take courage to tackle the tough questions, which are often more behavioral than operational.

- Address the behavioral issues in the context of the operational and while solving key business issues.

Notes

....

....

....

....

....

....

....

....

....

....

....

....

....

....

Chapter 4

The Ravine

Five am arrives sooner than expected. Dirk rolls out of bed and jumps in the shower, probably the last for several weeks. He gathers his gear, sorts it according to the checklist provided by Roger, and then carefully packs it into the various pockets of his backpack. Four large jeeps pull up in front of the hotel a few minutes before six. After packing each jeep with the gear of three people, the group heads to their departure point in the mountains several hours away. The jeeps swerve through the streets of Kathmandu, avoiding smaller cars and motorcycles. Pedestrians jump out of the path of the oncoming vehicles. The morning traffic jam has not yet clogged the streets, and they make good time.

As the team travels on the well-paved road leaving the Kathmandu valley, terraces barely clinging to the hillsides appear. Brightly colored rhododendron trees grow to nearly sixty feet, amid juniper, fir, larch, and birch. A morning mist obscures the mountain ranges, but Dirk can feel the presence of these giants looking down on him. In a single file, the four jeeps cross a large river heading farther and farther into the mountains. The scenery becomes more spectacular every minute. As the haze begins to loosen its grip on the countryside, white clouds and blue sky emerge. The wood and stone structures of small villages, interspersed with yellow rapeseed and mustard fields, cling to the steep walls of the valleys.

After close to 200 km, the group reaches a small village, the departure point of the trek. The group eats a quick lunch of Dal Baht, rice, lentils, and some vegetables. Then they are ready to head out. The porters and kitchen assistants join. To Dirk, Karl and Carlos, who have never been to the Himalayas, it feels strange to have others carry their gear. Marianne puts them at ease by explaining that Nepal has so much unemployment that paying porters a few dollars a day helps them quite bit.

The team leaves the small village on a trail heading north. Cows and a few water buffalo are grazing in the abandoned terraces. With a wide river below and the magnificent snow capped peaks in the distance, Lisa is overwhelmed. "What an incredible view. It's easy to see why they call this the roof of the world."

Equally at awe, Carlos replies, "It is humbling. Puts life in perspective, doesn't it?"

Spiders, with webs the size of hammocks, are casually going about their business. A chorus of cicadas pierces the majestic silence as butterflies swarm around the trekkers. The trail is a series of uphill switchbacks, which are easier to walk than the steep downhill trail on the other side. Knees take a pounding, but thankfully, the porters are carrying the heavy packs, and individuals are in good physical condition.

The entire team, trekkers, porters, and kitchen assistants arrive at the campsite almost in unison. They set up tents and have their first meal in the high country. After a vegetable soup, spaghetti, and bean dinner, individuals go off to their tents. Roger and Dirk are tent mates.

"What's with these insects?" questions Dirk.

"In the lower valleys, we'll hear them a lot. They're quite noisy. You did bring your earplugs, didn't you?"

"Actually, I didn't. I saw that on your checklist and thought, earplugs in Nepal, he can't be serious. Now I understand."

"Not to worry. I always bring extra."

Getting used to sleeping in a tent for the first time in a while, and acclimatizing to the temperature, most of the trekkers are a bit groggy in the morning. An uneventful breakfast of tea and porridge doesn't necessarily lift their spirits. The team follows the river upstream accompanied by the twitter of birds. There are numerous waterfalls cascading to the valley below on the steep sections of the trail. The team traverses a few wooden suspension bridges, not yet used to the bounciness of the crossings and watching every step. Most of the bridges have a few wooden planks missing, where the trekkers can see the river rushing by far below.

The last crossing of the day has people thinking about their personal wills. Stretching across the river, wider than a ten-lane highway, is one lone steel cable with a diameter not much larger than a quarter. The thunder of the river is deafening, making the earth shudder beneath its power. The only way across is in an elongated metal basket, formerly used by the mountain rescue service, hanging to the underside of the cable. One by one, each trekker lies down in the basket and is pulled across the raging river by slow, cruel jerks on a pulley. With the utmost confidence in Roger and Bikram, individuals wager across. Close to dusk, the entire team is on the other side.

At dinner, they relive the story of the crossing, imagining how hard it will be to share the sensation with anyone back home. They head off to their tents, exhausted from a full day of hiking and the barrage of experiences.

The next day, the group heads out early. The porters and kitchen crew will pack up camp and then catch up by lunchtime. The trail is uphill and steep, leaving the river far below. Close to noon the team rounds a big boulder, and disaster strikes. The trail crosses back over a narrow section of the river; but the old, decrepit suspension bridge is out.

"Damn," Roger swears. "I have never heard of this bridge being out."

They are standing at the edge of a sheer cliff, staring across the deep mountain gorge. The river is one hundred feet below careening off the rocks. One of the main support ropes has frayed and sheared off. The wooden planks making up the surface of the bridge now dangle to one side. The team decides to break for lunch and discuss the various options.

The itinerary had been established weeks in advance; and up to this moment, it seemed perfect. Now, however, everything was in jeopardy. The team is visibly concerned but recognizes that neither Roger nor Bikram could have known about the bridge. In fact, what no one knows is that the last rope frayed the day before so the bridge has been out only one day.

Since this has a significant impact on the direction of the trek, Roger discusses the various options. "We can turn back and down in the valley take another trail, but it would mean a major change in the itinerary. We can see if there is a detour and hike around the gorge. Or we can try to fix the bridge."

He engages the entire group in a dynamic and at times heated discussion. He asks individuals to challenge one another's thinking and to look at the pros and cons of everyone's ideas. The discussion goes back and forth about the various options. No one's ideas are sacred. Individuals even challenge Bikram, who is the local expert. Individuals assess and build on each other's ideas. Roger interjects only periodically to keep the conversation moving. He spends most of the time listening to the advice and suggestions of the others. He uses the agreed upon ground rules to keep the discussion focused on debating the options and not attacking individuals. Roger's role throughout has been to prompt the group to openly voice their viewpoints, to discuss their ideas, to get them to test each others' thinking, and to make sure that the dialogue didn't get out of hand.

Dirk is quite surprised at the intensity and directness of the conversation. After almost thirty minutes, as the leader of the group, Roger brings the discussion to a close. "This is great; it gives us a good idea of the pros and cons of the various options. I appreciate people's candor and willingness to speak freely and challenge each other's thinking." Roger makes clear that as the leader, he has the decision-making authority. He is looking to the others for their best thinking and for their advice to him on what they think is best for the entire group.

He reinforces what they discussed in Kathmandu. "We all have to be able to commit to the decision even though we may not all agree. It's called disagree and commit. It's important to understand that maybe we cannot all agree 100%; but if we find a good solution for the whole group, we will all have to stick with it, commit to the implementation, and pull in the same direction." After explaining how he arrived at his decision, he lays out a course of action. "I've heard all your ideas and here is what I think we should do." He goes on to explain his rationale, its implications, and then asks each person to commit to the proposed course of action. All commit to the solution.

Sam, the best climber, crosses the gorge on the remains of the existing bridge. Then with additional rope, he pulls up the dangling planks and secures them. Two hours later, the entire group is safely across. A quiet sense of accomplishment begins to permeate the group as they continue to move higher and higher into the mountains. Everyone feels the confidence that comes with success.

The group continues along the narrow trail for another hour. They are in high spirits by the time they reach the campsite. The group pitches tents and prepares for the cold night. Karl jokes, "A few vegetables and this local bread, and this hot stew will be like a home cooked meal."

Lisa cheerfully adds, "Even with that little mishap, we still made it to camp before night fall."

Dirk thinks to himself, this little mishap, as Lisa put it, could have been a major setback. Even though they had a clear plan, this latest circumstance could have dramatically changed the entire trip. Yet, Roger led the team through making a major strategic decision that they all committed to supporting.

After dinner and small talk reliving the day's events, Roger reminds people not to leave anything wet outside. Anything left outside will turn into a popsicle. He tells of how on one of his first treks he had washed his underwear and left it hanging on the tent pole in the icy air. The next morning it was as solid as a wooden board. Lucky for him he had a spare; otherwise, it would have been an interesting day of walking. The team spends a few more minutes joking and giving one another a hard time. Then as the fire dies down, they head off to their tents.

Dirk climbs into his bright red mummy bag and in the dim light of the kerosene lamp takes out his journal.

Fourth Insight

Be ready to change the itinerary by making good, fast, strategic decisions.

- ➤ Realign the organization to changing circumstances.
  - Clarify changes to priorities and strategies, if any.
  - Honestly discuss changes and implications as a team.
  - Focus and mobilize the entire organization on the new direction.
- ➤ Get the best thinking on the table.
  - Create an environment of trust, open and honest debate.
  - Do not avoid conflict. Bring it to the surface.
  - Make sure that people understand they are advising you with what they think is best for the group.
- ➤ Clarify the decision-making process, so there are no hidden assumptions.
  - Ensure that people understand who has the authority for certain decisions.
  - Ensure that people have the ability to influence the decision.
  - Operate with a disagree and commit model.
  - Make sure that you reach closure: make the decision, summarize, explain the rationale, clarify the implications, and ask for commitment.

Notes

....

....

....

....

....

....

....

....

....

....

....

....

....

....

Chapter 5
Above the Tree Line

The team has now been trekking for a few weeks with a familiar pattern. Up steep inclines to a mountain pass, through the pass, and down the other side to beautiful valleys. Yak and cows often graze the steep hillsides with the villagers harvesting the fields. On occasion, the team encounters a barren landscape where landslides have wiped away houses and animals, covering good farmland with mud and boulders the size of small cars. The mountain passes are dramatic, bordering on the spiritual. Seeing clouds waft around the mountains makes each trekker take a few minutes, catch his or her breath, and enjoy the incredible vistas.

Up to this point the trek has been strenuous but not too difficult. There are challenging river crossings and narrow hillside trails, but as of tomorrow the trek will become a notch more difficult. This morning, like every morning, Roger calls the group together and outlines the day, explains the destination and the unique characteristics of the route. After a healthy breakfast of muesli and hot chocolate, Roger explains that from now on the terrain will be quite rough with the team crossing rock fields, consisting of loose rock debris deposited at the base of steep cliffs. They will also cross a section of a glacier and then finish the trek with a climb to the summit.

Roger points overhead to a small trail ascending skyward clinging to the side of the mountain. "Today we're going to hike a few hours up that trail to the base of a small ice field. There we'll set up camp. In the afternoon, Lisa and Larry will teach us a few lessons that could come in handy over the next few days."

Although some individuals are experienced trekkers, the team needs to master a few key mountaineering procedures. The first will be how to communicate with one another when several feet apart or in poor weather. The second is how to handle equipment such as crampons, harness, ice axe, tying knots and climbing ropes. The third is how to walk roped together, including making a glacial crossing.

The team breaks camp and heads toward what looks like a small stream. The suspension bridge is similar to the others they have seen. The stream, however, is forced through a narrow canyon which squeezes the water so tight resulting in a roar louder than that of a passing freight train. Marshall, underestimating the noise, tries to comment about the gorgeous waterfalls, but the deafening noise completely drowns out his words. Beth, a step away, only sees his lips move. They both realize how important it will be to master the communication procedure.

The team slowly makes its way up the steep switchbacks. Near the top, the trail becomes quite narrow, more ledge than trail. Individuals need to balance carefully, to find narrow handholds on the upward side of the rock. Small pebbles cascade off the side of the mountain as the trekkers take one careful step after another. Close to noon, drenched in sweat, the team reaches the ice field. Carlos mentions to Marianne, "I'm not sure I can get used to this climate. During the day, the valleys get hot and I sweat like crazy. As soon as we reach higher elevations, the mountains block out the sun and it's cold." Roger, overhearing the conversation jokingly adds, "Don't worry, Carlos. Soon it will be cold all the time."

As the kitchen crew sets up for lunch, Lisa and Larry prepare to explain the procedures and set up some practice exercises. After lunch, they begin. First, they practice how to tie knots, to hook and unhook one another to safety lines, even blindfolded. The team also practices walking roped together, which is not as easy as it sounds. At one point catching everyone off guard, Lisa pulls Carlos over and along the ice field simulating a fall. Not expecting the sudden tension on the rope, Karl, hooked to Carlos, topples over and begins to slide down the ice gaining speed. Lisa pulls on the rope and slows Karl's descent.

Karl slowly stands up and brushes the snow off his pants. "Good that we're only practicing on this small ice field."

Lisa explains that the rope between people must not be allowed to become too slack or too tight. If a person falls through a crevasse and the rope is too slack, he or she will fall too far. Too tight and the second person can lose his or her balance and be dragged into the crevasse as well.

"It is critical these safety procedures become second nature," Lisa says. "You've got to be prepared for the unexpected and know how to respond."

Larry continues, "Next, let's talk about our communication. Up here weather can change very quickly. When we walk along these trails, we may be several feet from each other and if there is wind or snow, it will be hard to hear. For the next few minutes I want to go over how we communicate in these situations."

The team then practices how to use an ice axe and walk with crampons. Lisa explains, "The primary purpose of the ice axe is to stop sliding on a slippery slope. We're going to practice 'self arrest' or 'ice-axe braking.'" She explains that when people fall, they tend to put their arms out wide. Instead, they should hold the ice axe firmly and get the pick into the slope almost before the slide has started. She demonstrates the technique and asks people to practice.

Individuals then strap on crampons. Larry explains, "Some of you are already experienced, so this is a review. When walking with crampons keep your body completely vertical to make sure all the points touch the slope. Your crampons will grip and you don't need to bash them in. Keep your feet apart to avoid entangling." He goes on to mention that the worst danger of walking with crampons is over confidence.

Teaching a group these techniques in such a short time frame is quite a challenge. To make it easier, Roger focuses only on those core processes that are necessary for the group to achieve their goals. In this case, that is how to communicate, how to handle the equipment, how to rappel and belay, and how to walk roped together. Everything else is secondary. Furthermore, a few team members are already familiar with the procedures.

To accelerate the learning, Larry and Lisa teach the team not only how to do the procedure correctly, but also how to do it quickly. It is about quality and time. By helping the team perform a procedure fast and correctly, individuals reach a level of fluency. Once people achieve fluency, it becomes second nature; and they will be able to respond in an emergency quickly and efficiently.

Dusk slowly settles over the plateau. With tents right next to the ice field, the night air is significantly colder. Dinner is hot noodle soup and Dal Baht, this time over chili. Exhausted after all of the practice, team members are in their sleeping bags by seven. Yet, because of the altitude sleep does not come easily.

During breakfast, Larry monitors the two-way radio and listens intently to the weather report. The sky is a beautiful light blue with a few scattered clouds. Larry is scrunching his face as he listens. Finally, he arises from his crouch and wanders off to look for Roger. Later at the standard morning meeting, Roger summons the group and asks Larry to give a quick weather update.

With a trace of concern in his voice, Larry says, "Doesn't look good. Although monsoon season is over, the weather service anticipates a storm over this region in the next twelve hours. Most likely it'll reach us late afternoon or early evening. Don't know how long it will last, but it could go into the night."

As Larry finishes, a few individuals let out a loud sigh. After a good discussion, the team decides that since it sounds as if it won't be here for several hours, they should move on and try to reach the next village.

A few hours later, the trail becomes narrower. Individuals can no longer walk in pairs but must walk single file. The trail continues to wind higher and higher, hugging the mountain face on one side with a steep drop-off on the other. It's a spectacular hike with the valley floor far below. The group is pushing hard to get off the winding trail before the storm hits.

Seemingly out of nowhere, dark storm clouds appear, trapping the sun for minutes at a time. Dirk is always amazed at how quickly the weather changes in the mountains. Sure enough, before they can reach their designated camp, the clouds let loose.

The wind has picked up, blowing a mixture of ice, rain, and snow everywhere. Thanks to Roger's planning, members are relatively warm and dry in their gear. They have passed the narrow portion of the trail but still have a few steep and treacherous areas ahead.

The team, roped together, is carefully making its way over the rocky path with little rivulets of ice runoff crossing the trail and cascading down a fifty-degree slope. Not watching his step, Carlos steps into a rivulet, loses his footing on the ice, and slips off the trail. Instantly knowing what to do, Dirk and Sam plant their feet and arch their backs toward the upper slope. They stop Carlos's slide within seconds. With the wind howling, Dirk and Sam use hand signals to let Roger know that everything is under control.

With a few minor scratches from the sharp rocks, Carlos sits on a nearby boulder catching his breath. "Thanks. A bit close," he gasps.

"You still had a ways to go before flying with the eagles," jokes Sam with the humor of an experienced mountaineer.

"Ha. Ha," says Carlos, "I haven't seen any eagles up here lately. It's probably too high for them."

A couple of hours later, just as the group reaches the small mountain village, the storm lets up. The team stays in a series of small stone guesthouses. Taking advantage of the daylight, Dirk asks Bikram, "As we came into the village I noticed a small monastery clinging to the hillside. I'd love to go see it."

"You're welcome to go there."

Dirk takes a small fanny pack and quickly zigzags up to the monastery. He knocks, and a monk slowly opens the brightly colored door. The monk beckons him in. Dirk removes his shoes stepping on the creaking floorboards in his wool socks. The dim natural light underscores the age of the monastery. He stands reverently at the door as he looks at the Buddhist altar. The monk beckons him farther inside, guiding him to a place to sit. Dirk sits on the cold wood floor staring at the colorful hangings on the ceiling. The serene environment causes him to reflect on the past weeks where his thoughts about the pressures at work continue to wrestle with his desire to think of nothing at all. He thinks about how Roger's emphasis on a set of standardized procedures, proficiency in these procedures, and clarity of responsibilities was critical to the performance of the group. To calm his mind, he pulls out his journal and begins to write.

Fifth Insight

It is important to master a few key processes.

➤ Look at the business as a set of 3-5 core processes.

- Understand the inputs and outputs throughout the processes.

- Clearly define success for each process.

- Realize it is about time and quality, not "or."

- Train processes until "fluency" is reached.

➤ Work at simplifying and standardizing processes where appropriate.

- Clarify who has the accountability for key decisions and responsibilities throughout the processes.

- Eliminate waste and complexity where possible.

- Clearly define the objectives and benefits of improvement efforts.

➤ Ensure executive team works together to improve the key processes.

- Develop shared goals and measures.

- Reinforce that leaders need to be visibly involved in improving the processes.

- Realize that when improving cross-functional processes, they may come together only at the top. The executive team must be involved in making key decisions.

- Instill a sense of urgency and stay focused on desired improvement results.

- Ensure that there is a common method to solving problems.

Notes

....

....

....

....

....

....

....

....

....

....

....

....

....

....

Chapter 6

Across the Glacier

The next morning the team gets up a little later than usual. The sun is shining brightly, and Dirk is amazed at how the sun casts such long shadows. They finish their toast, eggs, and tea and get ready to head out. The porters and kitchen assistants will pack up the rest of the gear and meet the team at base camp.

Roger explains, "Most people think of glaciers as rivers of ice. And that is close to the truth. They are an accumulation of ice, air, water, and rock debris that because of its own mass can flow very slowly or very quickly up to thousands of meters per year."

Sam continues, "There are several hazards on a glacier, but today the main thing we have to watch out for are crevasses. These long fissures in the ice can be quite deep. The problem is that snow or ice bridges often cover them. A trekker doesn't know they are there and steps on a thin piece of ice over a gorge hundreds of feet deep."

Like a tag team, Roger chimes in, "In the summer months these crevasses can often be wet from the melting ice. So if a trekker falls in, he or she may soon be wet from ice melt; yet the temperature in the crevasse is still freezing. Hypothermia can set in quickly. So, let's not fall into any crevasses."

The team leaves the small village and heads up the valley. "It's nice to finally have a trail where more than two people can walk side by side," comments Karl.

"Yeah, makes this seem like a leisurely walk in the park, except for having to gasp for air," replies Carlos. Karl's optimism about the wide track soon ends as the team leaves the main trail. They reach another rickety suspension bridge with a few planks missing and climb across the river. The trail turns into a narrow and much less hospitable path. Loose pebbles from a small landslide make walking a bit treacherous. Individuals have to put away their walking sticks since the narrow path does not leave enough room. In certain sections, the edge of the trail is beginning to crumble. All have to concentrate so as not to misstep or lose their balance.

Soon they reach the edge of the large moraine field at the edge of the glacier and take a short break. "From below the glacier looked a lot smaller. Now I can't see the end of it," comments Beth. "Thank goodness we're not hiking all the way across."

"You can say that again," replies Marshall.

They spend a few minutes to eat granola bars and chocolate. Then Roger assembles the team and reviews what they learned yesterday and how best to cross the glacier.

"Our goal is clear. We need to cross the glacier before nightfall. There's plenty of time, but you never know. If you look out on the glacier, by twelve thirty or so we need to reach that large outcropping."

"I assume you'll be watching the time?" states Marianne in a rhetorical tone.

"Yes. I will be telling you to speed up or slow down, depending on the conditions and our progress."

Then Bikram, who has crossed this glacier before, gives an overview how to watch for and probe for crevasses. If they walk in, or close to, one another's footsteps, there should not be a problem. He reiterates how much slack needs to be in the rope between trekkers. He shows them examples of the right amount of slack, too much and too little. As a final comment he says, "This is the way it should be. Remember what 'good' looks like. When it changes, too tight or too loose, let people know right away."

Roger, confident that they are ready, asks Bikram to head out. He will be in the lead and Roger will be in the back where he can see how the others are doing. They circumvent a green lake the size of a baseball field with small miniature icebergs bobbing up and down.

The team then navigates across a large moraine field, consisting of rocks, dirt, stones, and ice as they make their way to the edge of the glacier. Since there is no trail, they have to be careful not to twist an ankle. As the team finally gets out on the ice of the glacier, Lisa and Larry help people put on their crampons and get their ice axes ready. The slope is steep enough to where someone could easily begin to slide. Individuals take a few steps to make sure the crampons sit correctly. Given the extensive practice the day before, most are quite comfortable walking on ice. Larry makes a few additional suggestions on how Dirk and Karl can improve their technique. As the team continues out on the ice, the anxiety level increases as they notice the minor avalanches cascading down the face farther up. Roger observes how a few trekkers are letting these small avalanches distract them from concentrating on the task at hand. Using the communication techniques they had mastered the day before, he reassures them that these avalanches cannot reach them and that they should focus on where to take their next step.

The team climbs steadily upwards on the rough and chilling glacier. The white, at times translucent, ice shimmers in the sunlight. After about an hour's climb, Bikram makes a sudden stop. He asks Larry to hold the rope tight. He gets down on his hands and knees, and then lies flat on his stomach probing ahead with his ice pick. With one big swing of the pick, the newly fallen snow gives way and reveals a four-foot wide 100-foot deep crevasse. As the group catches up to Bikram, he explains to Roger how he had seen the color of the snow change. With no alternative, the group has to find a spot to cross. Five minutes later Roger and Bikram find a section where the crevasse narrows to about two and one half feet. Jumping across a 100-foot deep, dark black gorge will be a new experience for most, even if it is less than a yard across. Everyone should be able to clear this section.

Bikram and Sam demonstrate the technique, jump first, and easily clear the trench. The others must first determine from which foot to launch and then practice the two-step technique. Each takes a jump in turn. Only Marianne and Roger are left. Marianne, although having trekked in the Himalayas before, has never been part of such a strenuous climb. She takes a deep breath, moves forward, and plants her foot. It is too close to the edge. Unexpectedly the side of the crevasse gives way and she tumbles down. Bikram and Sam on the other side are ready as the rope goes taught. She falls only a few feet. Her legs dangle into the darkness as her shoulders catch on the far side of the crevasse. Sam's vigilance and quick reaction keep her from falling any farther. Together Larry and Sam haul her out. She sits trembling on the snow. Roger, having cleared the crevasse soon after, comforts her and places Marianne between Lisa and Sam, the two most experienced mountaineers. Still shaken she is able to move on.

To everyone's relief, they reach their halfway milestone, the outcropping, almost on schedule. Looking back, they realize it took them almost three hours to cross 1500 feet across the crevasse field. After having walked on the ice with no mishap for the past half hour and after positive feedback from her companions, Marianne is regaining her self-confidence. The team stops briefly for a quick lunch and then moves on. Storm clouds are beginning to gather again, and the last thing they want is to be on the glacier during a snowstorm, no matter how minor. They still have at least another two hours to go. As they continue to cross the glacier, it becomes more and more challenging. Although this section is crevasse free, it is forty degrees steep in many places, increasing the risk of slipping. The snow is firm, and the crampons are gripping. Anytime people do not place their boots correctly, they receive a comment from the person behind. The entire team is highly alert and ready to help and give one another feedback. Even Roger and Bikram are not excluded. Dirk notices that although the situation is tense and requires immense concentration, people appreciate the instant feedback. They take it positively; they see it as help and not as a sign of criticism.

Soon the wind picks up noticeably, blowing fine, snowy ice everywhere. It has not started snowing, but visibility goes down to thirty feet and it becomes dramatically colder. Even with gloves and mittens, Beth's hands start to tingle. At most, people can see two climbers ahead or behind. They can no longer see their destination and have to rely on the individual in front of them to lead the way. They are able to communicate with hand signals and short tugs on the rope. Mumbling to himself, Dirk thinks, "Thank God, we're all following the same procedure."

Within a half hour, they all catch up to Bikram, who is standing at the edge of what looks like another cliff. In reality, it is the edge of the glacier. They now have to rappel down and will then be back on the trail. The team rappels down the side of the glacier with ease. After they are off the glacier, it takes them another half hour to reach the campsite. The wind is still strong, but no snow has fallen. They pitch their tents in the most protected area. Within the hour, the porters, who took a different route, arrive with the rest of the gear. Given the cold temperature, they set up a kitchen tent where the team will dine together tonight. Bikram jokingly says, "Tonight ladies and gentleman, our five star meal will consist of noodle soup, eggs, fried noodles, cabbage salad, and squash." The team applauds. Roger then congratulates Marianne for her determination and effort to get back in the saddle after the incident at the crevasse.

Before dinner is served, Dirk and Roger sit in a warm corner of the tent and talk about the day's events. Dirk muses over how what he learned on the glacier today has relevance in his day-to-day life back at the company. He searches for his journal, now a bit soiled and worn, and while Roger continues to talk, he quickly jots down a few thoughts.

Sixth Insight

Appropriate levels of control are important to stay on track.

- ➢ Manage to a handful of goals and key performance indicators that everyone understands and can memorize.

  - Use leading, lagging, and process measures.

  - Identify the top priorities and what will NOT be done.

  - Be careful not to change priorities randomly.

  - Evaluate more than one person on a measure to ensure cooperation.

- ➢ Ensure that you have real-time operating data on the measures that drive the business.

  - Manage with a handful of key reports.

  - Establish a baseline from which people can assess improvement.

  - Provide real-time feedback.

  - Create a continuous improvement mindset.

- ➢ Regularly review progress on a consistent and standard set of measures, and a portfolio of projects.

  - Keep a balance. Don't over-emphasize process and reporting at the expense of doing the work and achieving results.

  - Create an environment where people are willing to surface risks and problems.

  - Realize that positive feedback is much more powerful in reinforcing behavior than negative feedback.

➢ Acknowledge and reward successful performance.

- Consider tying rewards to a set of shared goals.

Notes

Chapter 7

Leaving Base Camp

Having ascended nearly 3000 meters the previous days, a few team members have mild headaches, requiring a rest day to acclimatize to the higher elevations. Roger calls the group together for the morning meeting and explains, "The schedule for today is simple. After a leisurely breakfast we'll walk through the moraines, practice a few climbing techniques, and enjoy the spectacular views." Given the nice weather, the campsite has a truly majestic view of the Himalayan mountain ranges.

At a pasture below the camp, two herders arrive with thirty to forty yaks and their young. Yaks spend almost the entire year in these high pastures raising their young. Although warm in the sun, the light wind makes the temperature, hovering just below freezing, seem a bit colder. Individuals are comfortable around the fire and take walks around the plateau bundled in down jackets. Roger and Dirk spend a little time talking about teams and organizations but are quickly drawn back to the spectacular Himalayan landscape. Aside from admiring the views, the day is uneventful.

During the night, a light snow falls on the tents, as several members still struggle with sleep. As they get up, a dense fog enshrouds them. "Except for the yaks and tents this could be London," comments Larry.

"I've never been this cold in London," replies Beth.

Roger pulls the team together for the early morning review. They have a power breakfast of porridge, eggs, and some hot noodle soup while huddled around the fire. If the fog lifts, they will ascend to the ridge crest and then follow the ridgeline across to the summit.

The team gathers the necessary gear for the daylong trip: day-packs, food, rope, crampons, and ice axes. If everything goes well, they will arrive back at the campsite before dinner. Constantly reinforcing the team's core value of safety in everything they do, Roger asks each trekker to pack his or her head torch. This will help illuminate the path in case they get caught by nightfall.

Beth, who has already made a few ridge crossings in the Himalayas, doesn't have an issue with the head torch. She has a problem with the ice axe.

"Roger, this axe is too cumbersome. It's only going to get in the way."

"It's a critical piece of our safety equipment. What happens if you begin to slide?"

"I won't. I can hold onto the rope."

Roger takes her aside, fully aware that the rest of the team is following this conversation. The discussion gets animated and confrontational. Beth tells Roger that she is not comfortable with the axe and doesn't want to use it. She is more concerned about jabbing herself with the pick than arresting a slide. Roger listens and understands. Yet he is also firm about his expectations. He tells Beth that if she is unwilling to get comfortable with the ice axe, she will need to stay at camp. Beth is clearly frustrated and upset.

They return to the larger group and Roger asks for everyone's attention, "Today's ridge crossing is going to have some very steep icy slopes. The ice axe is critical in stopping you if you happen to slide. That's why we spent time practicing this technique. You need to be comfortable with the axe."

All look at one another.

Roger, holding up the ice axe, continues, "For those of you who are not comfortable with this piece of equipment, you have two choices. We can take thirty minutes this morning and practice a bit more, or you can choose to stay at camp. Ice axes are mandatory in crossing this ridge."

Bikram reinforces Roger's message. Beth, Karl, and Dirk take up Roger's offer to practice. The rest of the team feels comfortable in using the axe.

The fog finally begins to clear, and individuals finish a quick packing session and final check of their equipment. Roger explains that this time he will be in the lead, and Bikram will follow at the end. As they get to the steeper sections, he will climb ahead and place the safety ropes where necessary. They begin with a leisurely walk across the plateau and then ascend a steep unrelenting slope. Fifteen minutes later, Roger notices Beth hiking without her axe.

"Beth. Where's your ice-axe?"

"Oh. I must have forgotten it as we were packing our gear."

"You remember what I said. To climb today you need your axe."

"I'm sorry. I really did forget."

"That's fine. But if you want to climb to the summit, you need to go back and get it. We'll slow down to give you a chance to catch up."

"But we're already underway. I don't know if I can catch up."

The rest of the team continues to notice the interaction.

"Beth. No axe. No climbing."

Beth scrunches her face, reluctantly turns around, and heads back down the steep trail. Lucky for her the descent only takes half as long. Everyone recognizes Roger's commitment to safety. They see the consistency between what he says and his actions.

The team continues along the serpentine trail as the fog begins to burn off. They see glimpses of the glacier they crossed only days before, looking so quiet and benign. The horizon is dominated by the massive mountains, taking turns showing themselves through the fog curtain. By mid morning, the team, including Beth who had quickly caught up, makes it to the starting point for the climb to the summit.

Now seeing the steepness of the slope up close, several trekkers, including Beth, wonder what they have gotten themselves into.

The team sets up at the base of the snow ridge and discusses the order in which people will climb.

Roger explains, "Not everyone has to go to the summit. Those of you who feel uncomfortable and not well because of the elevation can stay here. You have an amazing view from here as well."

All want to go for the summit. All are confident that they can succeed.

Roger begins to climb the hard packed ice. Slowly, one step at a time he shows the others how they should proceed. As he goes farther up, he starts to fix the ropes. As people look up toward him, he looks like a small action figure on a massive sheet of snow. Beth and Karl are filled with a strange emotion. In a weird way they hope that he fails to fix the ropes or to reach the summit. If he can't fix the ropes, they wouldn't be expected to climb and could stay comfortable at the base of the ridge. As Karl thinks about not ascending, he feels relief in knowing that he doesn't have to take the risk. Yet at the same time, he feels disappointment for even considering not climbing to the summit.

Roger anchors the ropes and then comes down part way to help others. He signals for Beth, the first in line, to begin climbing. Off she goes, making sure her crampons solidly grip the icepack. The ridge is two feet at its widest with fifty to sixty degree slopes descending on each side.

A little over two hours later, the entire team is on the summit enjoying the spectacular views. The team is excited and enthusiastic about what they have achieved. Roger, always careful to balance between being positive and becoming overly confident, tempers the enthusiasm of the group.

"We're not done yet, folks. Success is when we are all safely at our tents. The descent can be more treacherous than the climb."

No sooner has Roger finished his sentence, Karl trips on his crampons and looses his balance. The rope becomes taught, and he doesn't go anywhere. As he watches Karl avoid a potential fall, Dirk realizes Roger's emphasis on teamwork, procedures, discipline, controls, and commitment has allowed this team to reach an incredible summit.

After snapping a few more pictures, the team begins the descent. Given the steep nature of the ridge, the trekkers cannot walk down. They have to climb down backwards, letting the rope slide through their hands to control the speed. Good that they had practiced how to rappel and belay a few days earlier.

As the sun sets on the distant horizon, the team returns to camp. The kitchen staff has prepared another wonderful meal of Dal Baht, and the fire is roaring. Excited and exhausted the team sits around the fire reliving the day. With everyone safe, Roger commends the group for how they worked together and singles out individuals who did an impressive job in helping the team meet its goals. Everyone reached the summit.

Dirk, listening to Roger, reflects on how the team reached a new horizon literally and figuratively. This trek stretched the capabilities of most individuals, including himself. Yet the system that Roger put into place helped everyone excel.

After dinner Dirk pulls Roger aside. "Although there was some hesitation before climbing the last part of the ridge, you were able to get people to commit to moving forward."

"I didn't get people to commit. I only made it clear that I was committed to moving forward and helped them join me."

"That sounds very Buddhist. Fitting up here."

"Let me explain Dirk. People check for confirmation with their leaders before they do things differently. They will only internalize their own commitment and act on it after they have experienced the commitment of their leaders. They don't just look at what was said. There is an old martial arts maxim that states, 'Do not listen to the words, for they may lie. Watch the body, as the body tells the truth.' People watch their leaders' behavior, draw conclusions, and watch closely for any contradictory signals. In some cases, they will test you and watch to see what happens. If leaders fail the tests, members typically withdraw their own commitment and the status quo remains."

"You mean like Beth with the ice-axe."

"Exactly. Behavior sends a strong message. Had I let her go without the axe, it would have sent a very different message."

Dirk continues to listen to Roger and later pulls out his journal, beginning to write.

Seventh Insight

Leaders must first show a personal commitment to change.

- ➢ Realize that people will adjust their commitment to change based on what they see their leaders doing.

    - • Do not underestimate how much leaders set the tone for what is acceptable and unacceptable.

    - • It may be less about resistance to change and more that people are unwilling to commit themselves if a leader has not shown his/her personal commitment to change.

    - • Leaders must maintain a "Constancy of Purpose." Changing direction or priorities too often, or without a clear reason, causes people to doubt the leader.

- ➢ Understand that people will test their leader's commitment to the change.

    - • Failing these "leadership tests" will cause a change effort to fail.

    - • Ensure that the leader sends a clear, decisive message and the leadership team a clear, cohesive message.

    - • Recognize that the leader's behavior is often scrutinized more closely than others'.

    - • Realize that in any human system people look for direction from their leaders regardless of their own position or title.

Notes

....

....

....

....

....

....

....

....

....

....

....

....

....

....

Chapter 8

View from the Outside

After a decent night's sleep, people slowly emerge from their warm tents to join the team for breakfast. Team members admire the incredible sunrise through steaming cups of tea. The realization is slowly sinking in; their wonderful trek is slowly ending.

Tents and supplies are packed; equipment is made ready; the group heads down the trail with Karl several hundred feet ahead. Larry, Sam, and Marianne make up the second group. The remaining people follow with Roger in the back.

About an hour into their hike, the trail makes a sharp right hand turn descending steeply around a large granite boulder the size of a small family home. They lose sight of Karl as he rounds the corner. A few minutes later the rest of the group clears the boulder. But there's no Karl. They look down the trail—nothing. Before they can yell, they hear him.

"Sam, Marianne, down here!"

Marianne and Sam can't quite place his voice. A few seconds later as they walk forward several steps, they see Karl fifty feet down a shallow incline. He is with four other trekkers, one lying on the ground.

"I need some help, quick!" he yells.

Marianne and Sam scoot down the incline to the other group of trekkers. One of them is leaning against a shallow rock, using a bandana to stem the trickle of blood from a nasty head wound. Sam, trained in advanced First Aid, pulls out his safety kit, applies antibiotics to the cut, stitches it up, and dresses the wound. He also notices the man's leg; bent backwards, a sure sign that it is broken.

Sam, Marianne, and Karl help the other three bring the injured man up the incline and back on the trail.

Roger decides to set up a makeshift camp for a few hours and asks the team to prepare food and drink. They set up one of the tents and put the injured guide inside. The others, although a bit battered, look fine, and in decent spirits. As they prepare the meal, Roger asks Phil, Monica, and George, the other trekkers, to fill him in on what happened. He also asks Larry, who is responsible for monitoring the two-way radio, to see if he can get help. Unfortunately they are in a section of the mountains where communication with the outside is nearly impossible.

Phil describes how they were heading back from a ten-day tour. Monica wasn't feeling well. The altitude caused her to become nauseous, and she had difficulty breathing. Their guide, Ralph, decided it would be best to take a shortcut to get her back more quickly. This required climbing down a steep rocky incline. They didn't have all the necessary equipment. Although they had all been trekking before, they were not clear about the techniques or standard procedures for such a climb. Their guide climbed down first. He was about thirty feet from the bottom when the rocks broke loose. He had not been anchored by a rope. He slid about thirty feet and then fell off a small ledge.

Roger chimes in, "Thank God it was only a few feet." Thoughtfully he says, "There's no alternative, you'll have to join our group for the time being. I'd like to spend a few minutes with Phil, Monica, and George, our new additions, and then we'll get together as a big group.

Roger condenses his group's Kathmandu preparation meeting into thirty minutes. Describing values and ground rules, he explains how the team operates. Rejoining the larger group, they spend thirty minutes introducing one another and then head out again.

For close to an hour the team hikes down the trail, passing forests of Daphne bushes with their sweet aromatic scent, pine trees, and rhododendrons. Larry tries the two-way radio again. This time he is able to get through, and the rescue service dispatches a helicopter. An hour later the helicopter arrives and picks up the injured guide. The remaining trekkers decide to hike out with Roger's group. As they walk along the side of the river, Roger's group looks up and sees the peak they have just climbed. Now switching back and forth across the river on the old wooden suspension bridges, the trekkers are actually enjoying the bounciness.

A few days later, they arrive at their destination. The village is one of the few with a small landing strip. Their small charter plane waits on a grassy clearing ready to take them back to the airport at Kathmandu. The trek is coming to an end. They all say goodbye to Bikram and his porters, thanking them for a memorable trip. Bikram with his dry sense of humor, says, "You will guide me next time I am a tourist in New York." All chuckle, as they squeeze into the charter plane. They will miss Bikram and the people of Nepal. The plane lifts off just a few feet from the end of the runway and ascends through the valley. The plane flies over the peaks, across glaciers, through beautiful valleys. Dirk is struck by how the miniature landscape now looks so tame. Yet for the past three weeks, this same landscape challenged them to no end. What an amazing difference in perspective! Looking down at the rough terrain, Dirk realizes how much the environment influences behavior. He also recognizes how much Roger shaped the atmosphere and culture of this trekking group so that they would have the means to successfully navigate the perils of the Himalayas.

The team has one more day in Kathmandu before heading back to the West Coast. Monica, Phil, and George's flight was cancelled, so they arranged to be on the same flight as the rest of the team. Individuals take the day and explore the city one last time, culminating with a wonderful Nepalese dinner at the Hyatt.

At eight in the morning the flight takes off. The trekkers occupy the first two rows in coach class. Roger sits alone a few rows behind in an exit row. For several hours individuals relive their spectacular adventure, describing not only the amazing scenery that is Nepal but also the manner in which each person grew as an individual. They overcame critical obstacles as a team with determination and finesse.

The new additions, Monica, Phil, and George comment how Roger's leadership is quite unique. Since they were with the group only a few days, they have an insider and outsider perspective. They are able to describe the uniqueness of this team in some detail—the cohesiveness and high level of trust, executing like clockwork, and making difficult decisions.

The others agree. They describe how from day one Roger built a climate of excellence. They give him credit for the success of the trip. Everything seemed so natural, flexible, and yet disciplined. They all agree that they would trek with Roger anywhere in the world.

Dirk, after listening to the group, takes his diet coke and squeezes by the food cart to sit next to Roger.

Roger is enjoying a gin and tonic and is looking at the beautiful cloud formations beyond the wing. Occasionally he glances into his novel.

As Dirk approaches, Roger looks up. "Hey, Dirk."

Dirk lowers himself into the aisle seat, "After hearing the conversation up front, I just had to talk with you."

"The conversation up front?"

"Yeah. I've never seen such an enthusiastic group. You orchestrated a great tour."

With a genuine sense of humility Roger replies, "It was a good group, and others could have done just as well."

"You created an environment that brought out the best in people. It was interesting to hear an outsider's perspective from the other trekking team."

"Well, thanks."

Thinking about his business, Dirk continues, "My guess is you created that type of environment at your companies as well. The results speak for themselves."

"Luck had something to do with it. The markets were good. Remember when I was building those companies, I stumbled a lot."

Dirk adds in a probing manner, "But you did make it happen."

"You're still looking for that silver bullet, aren't you?" Roger quips smilingly.

"If there is one?"

"Nope. If you address both the leadership and operating practices, you can begin to see a change in the culture."

"Culture?"

"When we started this trip, we had a group of people that came from different places, had different values, and looked at the world through different lenses. Given what we wanted to accomplish, we had to make sure we were all on the same page and lived up to the same core values."

"So that's why you took the time during the first day to clarify values, ground rules, and our itinerary?"

"Yes. A core value was safety. So I tried to reinforce that value in what I did, with the goals, with the measures, with the procedures."

"I can understand. All the pieces have to tie together."

"Right. And when we talk about taking a company to the next level, it is about changing the culture. Let's say from a family to a more professional orientation. From the avoidance of conflict to dealing with conflict. From a loose management system to a more systematic one."

"I hear people talking about values and culture all the time, but it all seems a bit fuzzy," counters Dirk.

"It doesn't have to be. Decide on the culture you need in order to reach the next level and then look at the leadership and the operating practices."

"You mean like decision-making, the team, metrics, rewards, control systems?"

"Exactly, those all influence culture."

"I see," mumbles Dirk.

As the drink cart passes, Dirk slowly gets out of his aisle seat next to Roger and stretches to loosen up his weary body. He heads back to his seat to take a short nap. But before doing so, he pulls out his journal.

Eighth Insight

Leaders are responsible for shaping the culture.

> ➤ Define and/or clarify core values.

- • Understand how current values have led to success.

- • Determine if there is a difference between stated values and actual values.

- • Understand how current operating practices (e.g., strategy or operations review meetings, decision-making, goals, reward and recognition system) reinforce core values.

> ➤ Define which core values you need to modify or add, to reach the next level of growth.

- • Revamp operating mechanisms to support the values.

- • Translate core values into operational specifics.

> ➤ Realize that culture can be modified, but that it is highly resilient to change.

- • Recognize that passing leadership tests becomes critical when beginning to change the culture.

- • Recognize the importance of a compelling vision, mission, and clear strategies to help people understand where the organization is heading.

- • Make sure that vision, mission, and strategies (how something is going to get done) are clear and operationally defined.

Notes

Chapter 9

Back in the Trenches

The first week back at work Dirk does nothing but catch up on email, voicemail, and deal with the most pressing issues. He hasn't had much time to reflect on the trek, but his journal lies on the corner of his desk. On the weekend, ten days later, he finally catches his breath and picks up his journal with the eight key insights from his trip. Sitting at his patio table, Dirk reviews his journal notes and jots down a few next steps—his one-page plan for taking his business to the next level.

<u>Eight Insights</u>

1) Empathy is at the heart of customer loyalty.

2) The team at the top must lead as one based on a clear itinerary.

3) Leaders need to take an honest look in the mirror.

4) Be ready to change the itinerary by making good, fast, strategic decisions.

5) It is important to master a few key processes.

6) Appropriate levels of control are important to stay on track.

7) Leaders must first show a personal commitment to change.

8) Leaders are responsible for shaping the culture.

<u>Eight-Point Plan</u>

1) Strategic planning process—Clarify priorities for technologies, services, markets, and customers based on market and customer feedback.

2) Executive team alignment/communication—Work with senior executive team to improve alignment and decision-making. Model the behaviors necessary at the next level of growth. Drive decisions as a team.

3) Core processes—Streamline and improve three to four core cross-functional processes. Ensure cross-functional collaboration and process discipline.

   a. Go-to-Market and new product development (Customer need to release).

   b. Cash flow issues. Supply chain (Quote to Cash).

   c. Improving the conversion rate from lead to orders.

4) Real-Time Data—Agree on a handful of key reports, ensure real-time operating data even if the systems aren't ready. Review these measures consistently every month in operations review meeting to track improvement.

5) Executive Dashboard—Develop a handful of leading, lagging, and process indicators.

6) Goal Alignment—Look at executive and director goals to ensure alignment, eliminate any conflicts, and develop a few shared measures.

7) Improvement Projects—Manage improvement efforts as a portfolio of projects.

8) Operations Review Meeting—Revamp the operations review meeting to become the key forum to initiate and review changes in operations, projects and make decisions.

Satisfied he leans back and contemplates how he's going to introduce his new ideas to the management team. His momentary peace and quiet is interrupted by a phone call from none other than Roger. He happens to be in town and is free for dinner. Happy to see a good friend, Dirk accepts the invitation.

They meet at a small rustic restaurant just off Highway 280. They exchange pleasantries and talk about their families for the first half hour. Before the main course Roger asks, "So how's the business?"

"I've been so busy catching up. I haven't given much thought to what's next. Yesterday afternoon was the first day I actually managed to find some quiet time to think about what I'm going to do."

Dirk then goes on to describe his plan. Roger, as always, listens carefully and nods.

After Dirk finishes, Roger leans back and in a serious tone says, "Dirk, you have to know why you want to do this—deep down."

"I know it's going to be hard work."

"As I mentioned on the trek, it is more than hard work; you will be tested in many ways. For example, when I confronted one of my VPs, his wife went to my wife, who then questioned me at home. You have to be ready for that and more."

"If you are not clear on why you want to do this, if the energy and courage are not coming from somewhere deep inside you, you won't have the resilience to fight the battles. Things are going fairly well. The business is profitable. You and Mary don't need the money. You could get out now and travel the world for a while. Matter of fact, most of your management team probably doesn't need the money. Nothing is that broken, so why do anything?"

Dirk, sipping on his Merlot, casts his eyes off into the distance. "I'll tell you why. We can be the best. Our technology can change the way people work."

With passion, Dirk describes his vision—why he started the company in the first place and his goals.

He then summarizes, "Most importantly, I want to prove that I can do it. I want my legacy to show how I was able to take this company and build a great company that will last for years to come."

Over the main course Dirk and Roger continue to talk about Roger's experiences in the trenches of implementation. They talk about the political dynamics of getting key individuals from his staff and advisory board on the same page. Roger had to manage a Board of Directors. They talk about how to educate key stakeholders. Roger suggests that it might be best to focus on a few specific measures, to form a regular operations review meeting with open honest dialogue, to align goals, and then to look at the how and where decisions are made.

They top off their dinner with a glass of Cognac and talk about other things besides work.

Heading out to their cars, Dirk shakes Roger's hand, "It was great seeing you again. Thank you."

"For what?"

"For your ideas. You always force me to step back a bit and reflect."

"That's what friends are for. Give my best to Mary."

"Good night Roger. Hopefully, we'll see you soon."

The Beginning

Several days later, on a Thursday afternoon, Dirk is in his office, thinking about how to accelerate his business's transition. To obtain more input he decides to talk with two key advisory board members and three of his executives. Dirk trusts them implicitly, and they have all on occasion voiced their concerns about how to best grow the business.

Dirk asks his assistant to schedule a separate dinner meeting with each of the individuals, starting with the two advisory board members. Each meeting has roughly the same agenda. Dirk talks about where things are breaking down in terms of customer service, delivery times, product quality, and the ability of the company to read the market. He describes his hypotheses as to why things aren't working. As the others talk, he spends a considerable amount of time probing and listening. Do they see the same problems and underlying causes? Do they agree with his assessment? Dirk describes what their support would look like and then asks for their commitment. He helps them understand how leadership will be tested and how passing these tests will be critical to moving the business forward.

The conversations are both casual and intense. Each knows how challenging it is to change the basic operating practices of a business; however, they are convinced that making these changes is the right thing to do.

Several days later Dirk asks one of these executives to help pull together any existing customer and operating data that describe how the business is doing, customer surveys, partner surveys, etc. He decides to spend more time with a cross section of customers and employees. Normally spending time with the large accounts, this time he decides to spend time with the smaller up and coming customers as well. He talks with suppliers and channel partners, both big and small. He also schedules several small group meetings with employees. The agenda for each of these meetings is simple. Dirk listens to what is not working today and to how the business can be more efficient and effective. He asks a few critical questions and then actively listens, pushing and probing to get the real answers. Too often partners or customers, afraid of losing the business, don't provide the real story; or employees afraid of possible retribution cite only minor problems. He reassures them that he wants to know what is really happening. During each of these meetings, he brings along an assistant to analyze all the information and to consolidate the learning. On occasion, he takes along other executives.

After about eight weeks Dirk has a good picture of what the business is doing well and its biggest challenges strategically, operationally, and culturally. Patterns have emerged. As the company's foremost cheerleader, he needs to strike a balance between appreciating what the company has done so far, and motivating the organization to make a few key changes.

During the next executive staff meeting Dirk talks about what he has learned from his discussions with customers, partners, and employees. He acknowledges that the business is doing fairly well and that everyone should be proud; however, customer expectations are rising. They are becoming more and more demanding, less willing to tolerate problems. Competition is heating up on two fronts—the startups with their ability to innovate and the big industry players.

He cites the growing pains that the executive team needs to address to grow the business. The bar is rising. There are early indications that as they encounter more competitors they will have to operate differently. He notes how people are always too busy and constantly fighting fires; how there is duplication in effort; how people do not know who has the authority for certain decisions; how it takes too long to solve cross-functional problems; how cycle times are increasing, and how product and service quality are beginning to deteriorate.

Several executives feel that there are a few minor hiccups but that in general everything is going well. Others see more issues. Some do not say much at all. Dirk ends the meeting stating how he would like to handle the next executive meeting. He would like to schedule it on a Friday afternoon, and to double its length in order to discuss the findings and issues in more detail. The group discusses a few more agenda items. The meeting then adjourns with some of the people wondering what has gotten into Dirk. Maybe it's another 'flavor of the month,' or Dirk's newest priority.

Two weeks later it is a beautiful summer day, and half of the executive team wishes that they could go home early to enjoy the afternoon with their families. Of course, that rarely happens.

Individuals arrive within a few minutes of one other.

As they get settled, Dirk reviews the agenda for the meeting. He continues his introduction, describing his concerns. Not convinced, one executive replies that most companies undergo these growing pains and that there are problems but that the situation is not that bad.

Dirk listens to the other comments across the table. There are several one-on-one responses replying to Dirk's questions, but actually there is little true dialogue or debate. Executives are hesitant to tread on someone else's territory or to challenge one another too vigorously. They know that when it is their turn, the favor will be returned.

Dirk wants to improve how they work as a group. He realizes that this will take time and that it will need to be done one step at a time. He then redirects the conversation to look at the customer, partner, and employee data.

A handful of executives are still not convinced; however, it is their boss's meeting.

Although they have done surveys before and have tracked customer satisfaction and other measures, the data is eye opening, especially since Dirk and the other executives have probed beneath the stated responses. The qualitative comments are so consistent and piercing. There were also comments directed toward the executive group, revealing how they often were not on the same page or how they often gave conflicting direction.

But the business has also done many things well to reach this size. They need to acknowledge the past. Now, however, it is about succeeding in the future. To keep their energy focused Dirk talks about the need to change the way of thinking. The executive team needs to visualize how the business has to operate at the next level. As an example, what would have to be in place for them to manage twice the sales, improve product and service quality—all with limited increases in staffing levels?

Dirk pulls out his eight-point plan as he says, "I've jotted down a few items that I think we should address."

The team takes the next hour to discuss the details of Dirk's eight points. Dirk asks each member of his staff to sponsor one improvement effort. He intends to revamp the executive operations review to consistently review a standard set of financial and operating measures and progress on these improvement initiatives. On one hand, he just wants to tell them this is the way it is going to be. Yet on the other hand, he is trying to model the behavior of soliciting input and facilitating an open discussion. He makes it clear that the sponsors are accountable for the success of the initiative and need to provide the update to the rest of the executive group. He deliberately asks executives to lead improvement efforts outside their area. He wants his executives to begin looking at the entire business, to look at the business through his eyes, not just their functions.

The day is slowly winding down, and the group is becoming tired. Nevertheless, there are still a few items to discuss. One is what to do with the various committees and teams that are currently leading improvement efforts. They seem to be adding to the confusion as to who decides what and to the duplication of effort. Dirk suggests that they reduce the number, clarify their authority and their charter, and understand how these councils tie into the current structure of the organization. He asks the VP of Finance to make a recommendation of how to revamp the councils and teams at the next operations review meeting.

They then discuss the challenges of execution and implementation and the important role senior management has in setting the tone and "walking the talk." Dirk spends ten minutes describing how executives will be tested as they begin to implement these changes.

Next, they agree on a common methodology on how to manage improvement projects. His intent is to begin managing these improvement efforts as a portfolio versus one-off projects. Each needs to clearly identify the problem which it is solving, the value of solving that problem, and the method of measuring success. It is also necessary to understand the root cause, to put together an implementation plan that can deliver results in less than six to nine months and to establish controls to ensure that the effort continues to deliver the results.

The group is now visibly tired and ready to call it a day. To wrap up the meeting, Dirk recaps the decisions, highlights the implications, and finishes by asking the members what they feel went well during today's meeting and what could be improved. He wants to implement a two-minute exercise at the end of every meeting to make sure they continuously improve how they work together. Not used to this exercise and tired, most just give a perfunctory answer.

As the group disbands, some are on board; others are neutral; a few are openly skeptical; and one or two think that this is a total waste of time.

Dirk has his work cut out, but he recognizes that he needs to take it one-step at a time. He also knows that he has to be careful about changing priorities too often—to maintain a 'constancy of purpose.'

A big challenge is to keep the organization focused on current initiatives and to keep the executives motivated. Given the day-to-day pressures and remaining fires, there is a tendency either to move on to other problems or to label something complete prematurely.

A few weeks later, the first two operations meetings are a bit rocky. At times Dirk falls back into his old behavioral patterns, coming to closure on issues faster than the group, or taking too much control over the meetings. He recognizes these issues and works hard at addressing them. He even asks for help in building his executive team and periodically includes an outside adviser in his staff meetings and operations reviews.

Several Months Later

The initiatives are not moving forward at the same pace. Those projects where executives are actively and consistently involved are showing results. The others are stalled or behind schedule. He remembers the conversation with Roger about how executives' commitment to change will be tested. If he doesn't confront the situation, it is actually a reflection on him.

Furthermore, improving the core processes is turning out to be more of a challenge than expected. Employees have to work more cross-functionally; this is new for many of them. Most of the employees still operate in the "old" way where they just do it themselves to get it done. This no longer works. To achieve results, changes in procedures or changes in behavior are required in several functional areas at the same time. And if executives aren't modeling integration, it makes it so much tougher.

They are making good progress in the new product development area. After a quick assessment, the executive team decided to launch a cross functional team sponsored by the VP of Marketing and the VP of Engineering. This team developed a framework of how to develop and launch new products and services. This team was responsible for designing a process that helped development teams consistently meet delivery dates, improve launch quality, and reduce time to profitability. Dirk wanted two sponsors to begin to show the need for cross-functional collaboration. Both were accountable for the results. They are also the ones that provided the progress update to their peers on the executive committee. A subset of the cross functional team would join for that portion of the meeting.

The team used a somewhat unconventional implementation approach. Normally in such large-scale improvement efforts, much time is spent in designing a new process, new metrics, and new procedures; the actual implementation does not happen for several months. At an industry seminar, however, the new VP of Engineering learned how this often causes problems even with the best of all intentions and can cause the best teams to fail. This occurs partly because the issues are often quite complex, and the team can never know all the pitfalls and issues ahead of time. If it waits months before ideas are tested, it may inadvertently be designing in some fatal flaws; consequently, this team used an approach similar to rapid prototyping. While the team is working hard at designing the entire process, it also tests the entire process in small, rapid experiments. This is different from quick hits in that it is testing the entire process with one product, one group, or one technology and then incorporating the learning into the larger design effort. Dirk wants to reinforce the value of seeing things as hypotheses that need to be tested versus facts. This was part of his third insight.

The results are remarkable. The first two development projects were only a few days late with all the requirements for launch complete. The VP of Engineering and the VP of Marketing are clearly communicating their expectations and have taken the concept of "leadership tests" to heart. The team is making significant progress. They are all measured on the same goals, work across functional boundaries, and have disciplined project management.

Unfortunately, not all is working so smoothly in sales. The conversion rate from leads to orders is appalling. Lead quality is actually quite good, but they are not being converted. There is no systematic way of tracking lead to order. Secondly, the sales process is undisciplined. Sales people devote most of their time to search for information, to handle administrative tasks, and to follow up on implementation issues, instead of closing deals.

Dirk has addressed this issue numerous times with the VP of Sales to no avail. He is not an operations oriented individual. He is more focused on strategic issues. His ideas have been significant in fueling the company's success. He also believes that he is in line for the CEO position. However, with his inability to address operational issues he is losing respect from the other executives, and the organization is beginning to question senior management's leadership capability.

Furthermore, to make things worse, some see Dirk protecting and excusing the behavior of a long-time colleague. Dirk is aware of the situation. He agonizes on what needs to be done and has numerous late night conversations with Mary and others. She reminds him how often he has talked to his VP about this issue and how many chances he has given him to improve.

After several days of working through various scenarios, he meets with his VP of Sales. Dirk lays out his concerns again and discusses moving him into a strategic role with only two direct reports. The VP sees the writing on the wall, but outwardly accepts his new role.

Dirk meets in person with all the sales people. He writes a memo explaining how the VP's talents are best used in a strategic capacity. The organization will search for a seasoned executive who can help implement the disciplined processes required to take the sales organization to the next level. The organization understands Dirk's struggle, but recognizes his commitment to change. Dirk passes an important test.

Three months later the former VP resigns and leaves. Not unanticipated, it still hurts. Dirk remembers that this is the personal pain Roger warned him about.

As the implementation of the major initiatives continues, there are other issues and tests that have to be overcome. A few executives talk about their concerns to board members. These board members confront Dirk at the next board meeting and question his plan.

At the next executive staff meeting, Dirk addresses the issue of not openly voicing concerns and tells them that part of open dialogue is getting the issues on the table. He also feels that bypassing him and the executive team and going to a board member is unacceptable. He mentions that he has no problem with executives talking with board members but that they should also be willing to raise the concern in front of him and the executive group. One particular executive was more interested in building his own powerbase and continued to politicize the situation. After the next occurrence, Dirk let him go.

Roger was right. This was not easy on many levels. However, Dirk feels invigorated. He knows what the business could be; he thrives on the challenge of building a world-class company; and he enjoys the personal development required.

Driving home on Highway 280 one evening watching the fog creep over the hills Dirk finds a moment to reflect on what helps him keep a steady hand on the tiller during these stressful times.

- The love from his family.

- His goal to build a great company and leave a personal legacy.

- His focus on providing value to customers.

- His dislike of complexity and waste, a need to keep it simple.

- His faith in, and desire to, bring out the best in people.

Chapter 10

A Pacesetter

Dirk is pleased. Quarterly results have been consistent. Profits are up. But this week was special. This week the most respected industry-wide benchmarking organization finished its review of fifteen companies in the industry. All industry players use this organization to gauge the effectiveness of their businesses versus their industry peers.

There is great news. The business was designated not only as industry leader, but also as a pacesetter—this against much larger competitors. They scored in the top five on seven key performance indicators while growing revenue 30% per year.

It wasn't without sacrifice. Any time quarterly numbers dipped, there were those who doubted his approach. He had to confront his own weaknesses as well as those of a few people who helped him build the business. He always treated people fairly and ethically and recognized what they had brought to the company.

Dirk knew that open dialogue would help his business make better strategic decisions and improve execution. But at times he was impatient and not always comfortable with the debates. However, he recognized his own shortcomings and made every effort to improve. His team saw how he made an effort to change his behavior and worked with him to make the transition. There were times the "old" Dirk would rear his head, but the team trusted one another enough and had evolved to a point where they could tell him directly.

He worked consciously at instilling new disciplines and operating practices at the top: strategic clarity, a dashboard that captured key operating metrics, effective operations review meetings, and a focus on operational excellence and continuous improvement.

Throughout the past eighteen months there were times when Dirk called Roger for dinner or for a brief phone call. It was good to have a sounding board on organization issues. Dirk always knew that he had the technical skills and business savvy. He appreciated Roger's experience with the intangible aspects such as organization, people, processes, and culture.

At the executive team's strategic planning session, Dirk decides to take a few minutes at the beginning to describe the results of the benchmarking exercise. It is clear that the executive team has pulled together. The composition is different from eighteen months ago since a few members were not suited to the transition and were asked to leave. Others moved into different positions, and a few new people joined who brought a fresh perspective.

Dirk displays a bar chart on the overhead, and there is a moment of complete silence. Not only are the key indicators all heading in the right direction, but also profit has increased. The chart clearly shows that they are setting the pace for the industry. Within seconds, individuals congratulate one another. Sitting back, Dirk watches how his staff immediately begins to debate the pros and cons of how best to communicate the great news to employees and to reward them for their outstanding performance. They place ideas on the table, joking and giving one another a hard time. He can see the trust and sense of teamwork. It is amazing when 'the pieces come together.' Watching his staff, he reflects on the eight insights he gathered in Nepal and realizes that he and his executives have taken the business to the next level. As he gets up, he is already thinking about the next peak.

Epilog

Choosing One Place to Start

As stated in the introduction, this fictional story is based on years of working with organizations and of observing what makes them work well or not so well. It is about taking an integrated perspective of both business and the more intangible aspects of leadership, organization, and culture.

Some may say *Business Beyond Base Camp* is an idealized version of what it takes to reach the next level. Although not a true story, it is based on truth. I have had the privilege of working with executives to conquer issues similar to Dirk's. Some have adopted these ideas and have achieved remarkable success; others have adopted only a few or none at all and have not been able to take their organization to the next level—in some cases they even failed to survive.

Where to start is usually the fundamental question. Since most leaders are caught in the day-to-day stress of growth, they rarely have the time to step back. There are many places to begin the transition. If, however, I had to choose a single place to start, it would be to look at one meeting—the operations review. If there is no operations review meeting, I would wonder how the executive team makes decisions together.

Operation review meetings are wonderful microcosms of the business and windows into the culture. The pieces either come together in the operations review meeting, or they do not: how priorities are established, how progress is measured, how resources are allocated, how much the senior team trusts one another, how decisions are made, how well the organization can implement and execute.

If there is one place to start, then begin by implementing or improving the regular operations review meeting. Ensure that it is efficient, effective, and decisive.

I hope that you have enjoyed the story and have gained useful insights for your own business. Good luck in taking your *Business Beyond Base Camp*.

Additional Resources

For a free download
An Executive Summary of the Eight Insights go to
www.nl-leadership.com

Additional Reading

CEO Tools, K. Kramers, 2002

Designing Cross-Functional Business Processes, B. Johann (Putz), 1995

The Dynamic Enterprise, L. Friedman and H. Gyr, 1998

The Dynamics of Taking Charge, J. Gabarro, 1987

Execution: The Discipline of Getting Things Done, L. Bossidy and R. Charan, 2002

The Five Temptations of a CEO: A Leadership Fable, P. Lencioni, 1998

Good to Great, J. Collins, 2001

Growing Pains: Transitioning from Entrepreneurship to a Professionally Managed Firm, E.G. Flamholtz and Y. Randle, 2000

The Guru Guide: The Best Ideas of the Top Management Thinkers, J. Boyett and J. Boyett, 1998

The Five Dysfunctions of a Team: A Leadership Fable, P. Lencioni, 2002

High Tech Startup: The Complete Handbook for Creating Successful New High Tech Companies, J.L. Nesheim, 2000

Improving Performance: How to Manage the White Space on the Organization Chart, G.A. Rummler and A.P. Brache, 1991

The Inner Work of Leaders, B. Mackoff and G. Wenet, 2001

Leading at the Speed of Growth, K. Catlin and J. Mathews, 2001

Lean Six Sigma for Service, M.L. Dirk, 2003

The Loyalty Effect: The Hidden Force Behind Growth, Profits, and Lasting Value, F. Reichheld, 1996

The Power of Alignment, G. Labovitz and V. Rosansky, 1997

The Power of Simplicity, J. Trout and S. Rivkin, 1999

Unlock Behavior, Unleash Profits, L. W. Braksick, 2000

The Value Creation Bible for the Mid-Market, H. Kibel, 2001

Why Entrepreneurs Don't Scale, J. Hamm, 2002

0-595-32294-8